❧ This Book Belongs To ☙

Name :

Phone :

Address :

Project Name :

Foreman :

Project No :

Date :

Day :

Visitors

Schedule

Problems

Safety Issues

Summary Of Work

Signature :

Employee	Trade	Hours	Overtime

Equipment On Site	No. Units

Materials Delivered	No. Units	Equipment Rented	Rate

Others

Notes :

Project Name :

Foreman :

Project No :

Date :

Day :

Visitors	Schedule

Problems	Safety Issues

Summary Of Work

Signature :

Employee	Trade	Hours	Overtime

Equipment On Site	No. Units

Materials Delivered	No. Units	Equipment Rented	Rate

Others

Notes :

Project Name :

Foreman :

Project No :

Date :

Day :

Visitors

Schedule

Problems

Safety Issues

Summary Of Work

Signature :

Employee	Trade	Hours	Overtime

Equipment On Site	No. Units

Materials Delivered	No. Units	Equipment Rented	Rate

Others

Notes :

Project Name :

Foreman :

Project No :

Date :

Day :

Visitors

Schedule

Problems

Safety Issues

Summary Of Work

Signature :

Employee	Trade	Hours	Overtime

Equipment On Site	No. Units

Materials Delivered	No. Units	Equipment Rented	Rate

Others

Notes :

Project Name : ....

....

Foreman : ....

| Project No : |
| Date : |
| Day : |

Visitors

Schedule

Problems

Safety Issues

Summary Of Work

Signature : ....

Employee	Trade	Hours	Overtime

Equipment On Site	No. Units

Materials Delivered	No. Units	Equipment Rented	Rate

Others

Notes :

Project Name : ______________________________________

Foreman : ____

| Project No : |
| Date : |
| Day : |

Visitors

Schedule

Problems

Safety Issues

Summary Of Work

Signature : ______________________________

Employee	Trade	Hours	Overtime

Equipment On Site	No. Units

Materials Delivered	No. Units	Equipment Rented	Rate

<table><tr><td align="center">Others</td></tr></table>

Notes :

Project Name :

Foreman :

Project No :

Date :

Day :

Visitors

Schedule

Problems

Safety Issues

Summary Of Work

Signature :

Employee	Trade	Hours	Overtime

Equipment On Site	No. Units

Materials Delivered	No. Units	Equipment Rented	Rate

Others

Notes :

Project Name :

Project No :

Date :

Foreman :

Day :

Visitors

Schedule

Problems

Safety Issues

Summary Of Work

Signature :

Employee	Trade	Hours	Overtime

Equipment On Site	No. Units

Materials Delivered	No. Units	Equipment Rented	Rate

Others

Notes :

Project Name : ____

____

Foreman : ____

| Project No : |
| Date : |
| Day : |

Visitors

Schedule

Problems

Safety Issues

Summary Of Work

Signature : ________________________________

Employee	Trade	Hours	Overtime

Equipment On Site	No. Units

Materials Delivered	No. Units	Equipment Rented	Rate

<table>
<tr><td>Others</td></tr>
</table>

Notes :

Project Name : _______________________

____

Foreman : _______________________

| Project No : |
| Date : |
| Day : |

Visitors

Schedule

Problems

Safety Issues

Summary Of Work

Signature : _______________________

Employee	Trade	Hours	Overtime

Equipment On Site	No. Units

Materials Delivered	No. Units	Equipment Rented	Rate

Others

Notes :

Project Name :

Foreman :

Project No :

Date :

Day :

Visitors	Schedule

Problems	Safety Issues

Summary Of Work

Signature :

Employee	Trade	Hours	Overtime

Equipment On Site	No. Units

Materials Delivered	No. Units	Equipment Rented	Rate

Others

Notes :

Project Name :

Project No :

Date :

Foreman :

Day :

Visitors

Schedule

Problems

Safety Issues

Summary Of Work

Signature :

Employee	Trade	Hours	Overtime

Equipment On Site	No. Units

Materials Delivered	No. Units	Equipment Rented	Rate

Others

Notes :

Project Name :

Foreman :

Project No :

Date :

Day :

Visitors	Schedule

Problems	Safety Issues

Summary Of Work

Signature :

Employee	Trade	Hours	Overtime

Equipment On Site	No. Units

Materials Delivered	No. Units	Equipment Rented	Rate

Others

Notes :

Project Name : ____________________

____

Foreman : ____________________

Project No :

Date :

Day :

Visitors

Schedule

Problems

Safety Issues

Summary Of Work

Signature : ____________________

Employee	Trade	Hours	Overtime

Equipment On Site	No. Units

Materials Delivered	No. Units	Equipment Rented	Rate

Others

Notes :

Project Name :

Project No :

Date :

Foreman :

Day :

Visitors

Schedule

Problems

Safety Issues

Summary Of Work

Signature :

Employee	Trade	Hours	Overtime

Equipment On Site	No. Units

Materials Delivered	No. Units	Equipment Rented	Rate

Others

Notes :

Project Name : _____________________________

Foreman : _____________________________

| Project No : |
| Date : |
| Day : |

Visitors

Schedule

Problems

Safety Issues

Summary Of Work

Signature : _____________________________

Employee	Trade	Hours	Overtime

Equipment On Site	No. Units

Materials Delivered	No. Units	Equipment Rented	Rate

Others

Notes : ____

Project Name :

Foreman :

Project No :

Date :

Day :

Visitors	Schedule

Problems	Safety Issues

Summary Of Work

Signature :

Employee	Trade	Hours	Overtime

Equipment On Site	No. Units

Materials Delivered	No. Units	Equipment Rented	Rate

Others

Notes :

Project Name :

Foreman :

Project No :

Date :

Day :

Visitors

Schedule

Problems

Safety Issues

Summary Of Work

Signature :

Employee	Trade	Hours	Overtime

Equipment On Site	No. Units

Materials Delivered	No. Units	Equipment Rented	Rate

<table>
<tr><td align="center">Others</td></tr>
</table>

Notes :

Project Name : _____________________________

____

Foreman : _____________________________

| Project No : |
| Date : |
| Day : |

Visitors	Schedule

Problems	Safety Issues

Summary Of Work

Signature : _____________________________

Employee	Trade	Hours	Overtime

Equipment On Site	No. Units

Materials Delivered	No. Units	Equipment Rented	Rate

<table>
<tr><td align="center">Others</td></tr>
</table>

Notes :

Project Name :

Foreman :

Project No :

Date :

Day :

Visitors

Schedule

Problems

Safety Issues

Summary Of Work

Signature :

Employee	Trade	Hours	Overtime

Equipment On Site	No. Units

Materials Delivered	No. Units	Equipment Rented	Rate

Others

Notes :

Project Name :

Foreman :

Project No :

Date :

Day :

Visitors

Schedule

Problems

Safety Issues

Summary Of Work

Signature :

Employee	Trade	Hours	Overtime

Equipment On Site	No. Units

Materials Delivered	No. Units	Equipment Rented	Rate

<table>
<tr><td align="center">Others</td></tr>
</table>

Notes :

Project Name :

Foreman :

Project No :

Date :

Day :

Visitors	Schedule

Problems	Safety Issues

Summary Of Work

Signature :

Employee	Trade	Hours	Overtime

Equipment On Site	No. Units

Materials Delivered	No. Units	Equipment Rented	Rate

Others

Notes :

Project Name :

Foreman :

Project No :

Date :

Day :

Visitors

Schedule

Problems

Safety Issues

Summary Of Work

Signature :

Employee	Trade	Hours	Overtime

Equipment On Site	No. Units

Materials Delivered	No. Units	Equipment Rented	Rate

Others

Notes :

Project Name :

Foreman :

Project No :

Date :

Day :

<table>
<tr><td>

Visitors

</td><td>

Schedule

</td></tr>
<tr><td>

Problems

</td><td>

Safety Issues

</td></tr>
</table>

Summary Of Work

Signature :

Employee	Trade	Hours	Overtime

Equipment On Site	No. Units

Materials Delivered	No. Units	Equipment Rented	Rate

Others

Notes :

Project Name :

Foreman :

Project No :

Date :

Day :

Visitors

Schedule

Problems

Safety Issues

Summary Of Work

Signature :

Employee	Trade	Hours	Overtime

Equipment On Site	No. Units

Materials Delivered	No. Units	Equipment Rented	Rate

<table>
<tr><th>Others</th></tr>
</table>

Notes :

Project Name :

Project No :

Date :

Foreman :

Day :

Visitors

Schedule

Problems

Safety Issues

Summary Of Work

Signature :

Employee	Trade	Hours	Overtime

Equipment On Site	No. Units

Materials Delivered	No. Units	Equipment Rented	Rate

Others

Notes :

Project Name :

Foreman :

Project No :

Date :

Day :

Visitors

Schedule

Problems

Safety Issues

Summary Of Work

Signature :

Employee	Trade	Hours	Overtime

Equipment On Site	No. Units

Materials Delivered	No. Units	Equipment Rented	Rate

Others

Notes :

Project Name :

Project No :

Date :

Foreman :

Day :

Visitors	Schedule

Problems	Safety Issues

Summary Of Work

Signature :

Employee	Trade	Hours	Overtime

Equipment On Site	No. Units

Materials Delivered	No. Units	Equipment Rented	Rate

Others

Notes :

Project Name : ____________________

____

Foreman : ____________________

| Project No : |
| Date : |
| Day : |

Visitors

Schedule

Problems

Safety Issues

Summary Of Work

Signature : ____________________

Employee	Trade	Hours	Overtime

Equipment On Site	No. Units

Materials Delivered	No. Units	Equipment Rented	Rate

Others

Notes :

Project Name :

Foreman :

Project No :

Date :

Day :

Visitors

Schedule

Problems

Safety Issues

Summary Of Work

Signature :

Employee	Trade	Hours	Overtime

Equipment On Site	No. Units

Materials Delivered	No. Units	Equipment Rented	Rate

www.ingramcontent.com/pod-product-compliance
Lightning Source LLC
Chambersburg PA
CBHW060951050726
47592CB00003B/1186